ISBN 0-9651034-0-4
Library of Congress Catalog Card Number: 96-92052

Book design and production: Bruno Advertising
Art Director: Rob Treutel
Copy Editor: Andrew Legg
Prepress services: Paragon Prepress

First Edition 9 8 7 6 5 4 3 2 1
Printed in the United States of America

TERRA NOVA PUBLISHING
24 Harbourtown Village
Gulf Breeze, FL 32561

The Island: A pictorial journey through the Isle de Santa Rose including Okaloosa Island, Pensacola Beach, Navarre Beach and Fort Pickens

This book is dedicated to those who have given of themselves in helping to ensure the protection of the natural environment of this Island, this country and our planet. To my wife Conna for her encouragement, then patience; to my daughter, Molly, may she be able to enjoy the beauty of the Island throughout her life; and to all Islanders, in residence or in spirit.

A portion of the proceeds from this book will be donated to Gulf Coast Environmental Defense for their efforts in helping to protect our coastline.

The ISLAND

A PICTORIAL JOURNEY THROUGH

THE ISLE DE SANTA ROSA INCLUDING OKALOOSA ISLAND, PENSACOLA BEACH,

NAVARRE BEACH, AND FORT PICKENS

PHOTOGRAPHS AND TEXT BY MICHAEL O'DONOVAN

TERRA NOVA PUBLISHING

We are drawn to the Island
As sure as the pull of the moon on the tides
An inner voice, a flow of salinity
A winged prayer that is answered
In the sound of the sea

CONTENTS

LEFT: Tiki carver Jeffery J.O. Wheelock plies his
trade. Stopping by to watch this master craftsman
at work is a popular Island activity.

It was over 30 years ago. I still recall the briny scent from the Gulf of Mexico as my family crossed the old two-lane drawbridge that led us to Pensacola Beach. It was the first trip to the Island for us kids, and my parent's tales of adventure on the sugar white sands and fishing right out the back door were finally becoming a reality.

They were both raised in Pensacola, so coming back to the Island was as exciting for them as it was for us. Over the previous weeks their stories of long walks on the beach, crystal clear water and star filled evenings had built our expectations impossibly high. How could anything measure up to their exotic remembrances?

Then the wait was finally over as we drove up the oyster shell drive to our cottage on the sound. Even before the door to our summer home was unlocked we kids were wet to our knees and totally enraptured. It was all true. This was unlike any other place on earth. We stood immersed in that magical feeling only an island can impart.

We had left the continental United States and were floating in the Gulf of Mexico. An *Island*, we thought. Removed from civilization and charged with adventure! A fantasy land where the rules from the "real world" didn't apply and anything seemed possible.

Many years have passed since that day, but time has not diminished our attraction to Santa Rosa Island. We come here because it differs from the mainland; the slower pace, the natural beauty, the colorful people. Things that make up that unique set of circumstances known as "island life." We're removed, both geographically and psychologically, from the routine and the familiar. Stand on the beach and gaze out at the boundless Gulf, and one can't help feeling liberated and released. The vast combination of sky, sea and sand conspire to throw wide the doors to our hearts and souls.

I invite you to peruse the contents of this book, on which I've worked nearly as long as I've called the Island home. It won't take long before you start feeling like that smiling, carefree child you always had inside you, scampering down the pristine shores of the Island.

LEFT: A Tallahassee point, believed to be 9,000 years old, lies atop a Swift Creek Indian pottery shard. Both were found on the Island. Due to its advanced age, the point is believed to be a ceremonial tool created long before the tribe moved to the Island; it was probably passed down from generation to generation.

SLAND ELEMENTAL

It's made almost entirely of pure quartz crystal washed down from the Appalachian Mountains. It's over five thousand years old, and the entire land mass is moving west at the rate of two feet per year. It's almost fifty miles of sand, sea and mystery. It's known as a "barrier island", with the windward side facing the vast Gulf of Mexico and the leeward side curving around a collection of bays, bayous, inlets and wetlands. In some areas, the dunes are as arid and barren as any desert; in others, the marshes teem with an incredible variety of wildlife. • Men and women have heard the Island's call since before recorded history. Aboriginal Indians camped here and harvested its bounty. Spanish soldiers marched through the dunes and founded settlements on its shores. Today boats and bridges bring people by the thousands to those same dunes for pleasure and relaxation. • We love the Island for many reasons. It's the salt in the air and the sand between our toes. The way the sun glints off the bay in the afternoon and that breathtaking moment when a dorsal fin breaks the water's surface. It's the endlessly crashing surf, soothing our souls into a peaceful reverie. It's the Island. Elemental.

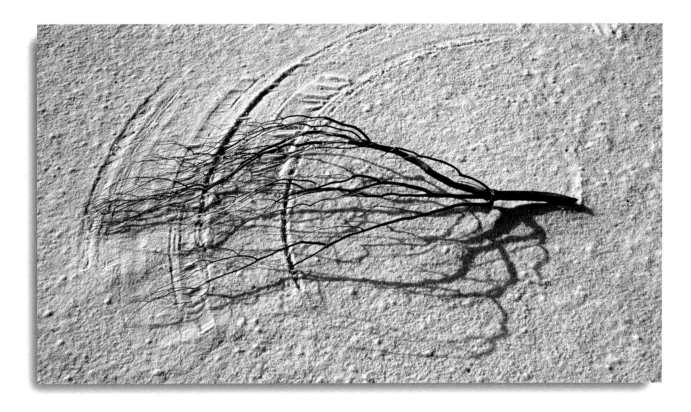

ABOVE: A wind-blown Florida Rosemary leaves its mark.

LEFT: Spectacular sunsets grace the Gulf during winter months.

ABOVE: Wind, water and weather combine to form a variety of hypnotic patterns. This "Island Art" changes from day to day and even from hour to hour.

RIGHT: The birth of a sand dune. Initially formed by hurricane winds, this young dune will need the help of vegetation for stability and continued growth.

ABOVE: *The same winds that build some dunes can erode, scour and diminish others.*

RIGHT: *Evening sky over a marina in Little Sabine Bay.*

LEFT: Dune crossovers protect the fragile dunes and lead thousands of beachgoers to the edge of the continental United States.

ABOVE: *A casualty of strong winds, high tides and weak planking.*

LEFT: *Windswept dunes near Fort Walton Beach.*

RIGHT: *A simple wooden mullet boat becomes a study in contrasts.*

LEFT: *Sand fencing is used to re-establish primary dunes weakened by both man and nature.*

ISLAND ELEMENTAL **23**

ABOVE: A driftwood skeleton is all that remains of a tree that once grew on this dune.

ABOVE: *The calm after the storm.*

LEFT: *A thunderhead looms ominously over the Intracoastal Waterway.*

The sea, once it casts its spell,
Holds one in its net of wonder forever.

- *Jacques-Yves Cousteau*

LEFT: Low winter sunlight casts
a silver sheen on the Gulf.

ABOVE: *A summer squall approaches from the south, creating whitecaps and an abandoned beach.*

I must go down to the sea again
For the call of the running tide
Is a wild call and a clear call
That may not be denied.

- John Masefield

ABOVE: *Moonrise near the cross commemorating Don Tristan De Luna's landing of 1559.*

ABOVE: *The name on the stern of a day-sailor perfectly describes this early evening scene.*

ABOVE: A portion of the "Sugar Bowl" dune preserve encroaches upon a wetland area.

RIGHT: Stands of seaoats are vital to the health of the Island's dunes. The root systems of these beautiful plants help prevent erosion all over the Island. Once picked in large numbers by visitors and residents alike, seaoats are now protected due to their importance to the Island's ecosystem.

LEFT: This dune, at the Gulf Islands National Seashore near Navarre, rises dramatically to a height of over thirty feet.

ABOVE: *January on the Island creates a different cast of hues over the Gulf, muting colors and light.*

LEFT: *High atop the "Indian Dune", a weather-worn oak remains anchored near ancient shell middens.*

At first glance the Island appears to be almost barren—miles of dunes, sparse vegetation and few areas that look hospitable to

wildlife. A closer look reveals a bustling eco-system that sustains an amazing array of flora and fauna. • A walk along the dozens

of marshes that dot the northern shoreline will lead to the discovery of imprints from an abundance or furry, scaly and feathered

creatures. These are our first clues to the wide diversity of animals who call the Island home. From the colorful green tree frog to

the majesty of the great blue heron, the Island offers a special cornucopia for the nature lover. The shores support a bustling

community of birds, fish, shellfish and much more. The nature trails of the Gulf Islands National Seashore are also an excellent

place to go wildlife watching, particularly for those seeking to catch a glimpse of the area's four-footed population. Sometimes

elusive but always fascinating, the nature of the Island is an attraction not to be missed.

ABOVE LEFT: *Hermit crabs find shells such as this one to call home.* **ABOVE RIGHT:** *Ghost crabs live up to their name, seeming to appear from nowhere then disappearing as quickly as they came. They also blend extremely well with the white sand on which they live.*

LEFT: *A dorsal fin breaks the water's surface. Then another, and another... a school of dolphin has arrived! There seems to be a natural and mutual attraction between humans and these playful mammals. Virtually all of the waterways surrounding the Island play host year-round to several varieties of dolphin. The best time to catch a glimpse of them is early morning or around sunset when the water is calm.*

ABOVE: *Green tree frogs are tiny but vocal Island inhabitants. Their chirping is heard everywhere after warm evening rains.*

RIGHT: *The red fox is rare, but still inhabits isolated areas of the Island.*

There is a pleasure in the pathless woods
There is a rapture on the lonely shore
There is society where none intrudes
By the deep sea, and the music in its roar
I love not man the less, but nature more

- Lord Byron

ABOVE: The raccoon constantly searches the water's edge for shellfish and other tasty morsels. Nestled in the safety of the dune scrub one also finds evidence of possum and even armadillo. Look for fairly large holes on the leeward side of the sound-front dunes, and you'll know you've found the nest of one of these delightful little bandits.

ABOVE: *Blue crabs are quick to defend their territory.*

LEFT: *Laughing gulls and brown pelicans share a perch. Gulls nest here by the thousands, taking every opportunity to beg a morsel from the Island's human visitors. Less abundant, but making a comeback, is the brown pelican. Once common along the northern Gulf Coast, the pelican population was decimated by the pesticide DDT in the 1970's. The pesticide caused their eggshells to thin, resulting in fewer hatchlings. Their return in ever greater numbers is a good example of sound environmental policy reversing dangerous trends on the island habitat.*

ABOVE RIGHT: *Sandpipers race along the edge of the breaking waves, endlessly outrunning the surf to catch shellfish before they burrow to safety in the sand.*

LEFT: *The largest bird on the island is the great blue heron. With a wing span stretching over six feet, these almost prehistoric birds are often seen wading in marshes or along the shorelines of our bays. They are wary of humans except at Fort Pickens, where fishermen have the birds practically eating out of their hands.*

ABOVE: A soundside marsh.

*RIGHT: Monarch butterflies rest on the Island before they
continue their annual migration from Canada to Mexico.*

ABOVE: *Migratory mallards chose a man-made lake on the Island for their year round home.*

LEFT: *Bouquets of indigenous dune flowers help stabilize the shifting sands.*

ABOVE: *Heavy spring rains bring a red-bellied turtle out into the open.*

LEFT: *Only from the air can the diversity of Big Sabine Point be appreciated. A major spawning ground for a variety of sea life, it also includes a pine forest, a major dune system and aboriginal indian sites from over 2,000 years ago.*

What is an Islander? It's more than just having an Island address. In fact, many "Islanders" don't actually live on one. It's less a permanent location than a constant state of mind. The "Islander attitude" sweeps over you when you leave the real world behind and enter that place of crashing surf and endless sky. It's seductive, irresistible. It whispers, urging you to forget your "respectable" lifestyle and return to the Island for a week, a month, forever. Answer that call just once and you're an Islander for life. • It's easy to spot an Islander. We wander aimlessly along the shore, smiling. We inspect unusual sea shells with great interest. We pedal rusty bikes into the sunset, heading to happy hour. We take great pride in fishing when the fish aren't biting. Islanders are masters at the art of doing nothing. Appointments, clocks and calendars give way to more natural rhythms: the rise and fall of tides, sunrise and sunset, the phases of the moon. • Island life renews us, takes us away from our ordinary selves. We are removed from the day-to-day routine and rejuvenated with fresh air, salt water, and simple pleasures. We slow down. A walk along the beach may take hours, but it's far from wasted time. Amid the sounds of surf and seagulls we begin to hear ourselves. That small inner voice becomes clearer, telling us to slow down a little more, to pick up that shell. We do, and while contemplating its textures and curves we discover an emotion hardly used since childhood— our sense of wonder. The time spent as an Islander is the best time you'll ever have.

ABOVE: Competing surfers await the
judges' verdict. Gulfside, late fall.

ABOVE: Sometimes more akin to flying than sailing, windboarders can skim the water's surface at speeds of 30 m.p.h. or faster.

Fishing tempts young and old alike to "drop a hook" in the Gulf, bay or sound.

LEFT: *Observers in Destin watch the start of the 100 mile "Round the Island" race, one of the longest multi-hull sailboat races in the country.*

*ABOVE: Shrimpers ply
the Intracoastal Waterway
near Deer Point.*

*RIGHT: Netfishing off the Island
has been popular for over three
thousand years.*

ABOVE: *A sand castle in Little Sabine Bay. Such temporary masterpieces are destined to disappear with the rising tides.*

LEFT: *A Mardi Gras parade adds a touch of New Orleans to Pensacola Beach.*

ABOVE: Island style trolleys ease traffic congestion on Pensacola Beach by providing free, casual transportation to all who step aboard...

RIGHT: ...while a more adventurous mode of transport is preferred by some thrill-seeking Islanders.

ABOVE: Wade Oceola, a Seminole Indian, attaches palm fronds to a traditional thatched roof in Navarre.

RIGHT: Music lovers flock to the Island to enjoy a wide variety of live entertainment.

We live in an old chaos of the sun,
Our old dependency of day and night.
Our island solitude, unsponsored, free
Of that wide water, inescapable.

— *Wallace Stevens*

LEFT: *The dazzling hues of Destin. These exotic, colorful waterways on the easternmost tip of the Island led to the area being dubbed "the Jewel of the Emerald Coast".*

Hurricane Opal left its mark on the Island in many ways. Gone are most of the Gulf-front homes from the 1950's, miles of roadway, and decades-old dunes. The unflagging spirit of the Islanders prevailed though, and today Santa Rosa Island, survivor of dozens of hurricanes since Luna's time, is more vibrant than ever.

SPANISH BEGINNINGS

It's the summer of 1559, and the New World beckons. Spain, ever seeking to expand its empire, is in the midst of a flurry of ambitious expeditions. One such journey is led by Don Tristan De Luna, an aristocratic adventurer known to be a religious man and a hard working leader.

Luna sets sail from Mexico with 1,500 passengers including soldiers, sailors, women and children, blacks, and even Aztecs. The 11 ships are well provisioned and hopes are high for establishing a permanent settlement in "La Florida" along the banks of the Bay of Ochuse - now known as Pensacola Bay.

LUNA'S LANDFALL

On August 14th the Island later proclaimed the Isle de Santa Rose comes into view. Upon making landfall the very first act of the expedition is to hold a religious service near where they landed on the Island's west side. This site is still marked with a cross commemorating the event.

The idea is to make the settlement Spain's linchpin in its bid for expansion in the New World. But the expedition is plagued with difficulties from the outset, and just days after reaching the Island a hurricane decimates the fledgling settlement. Almost all the ships are lost, including the main supply vessel. Gone is their precious supply of meats, cheeses and wines. Gone are the weapons and the tools. Gone, too, are Spain's dreams for a capital city in Northwest Florida.

THE END OF THE BEGINNING

Three years of hardship and misfortune follow for the unlucky explorers. Since the Indians are afraid of the settlers, no trade pact is established. The group never learns about the abundant food sources on which the local people thrive. Mutiny, rebellion and desertion are constant worries for Luna. Disease claims many who survived the storm. Of the original 1,500, less than 300 eventually return to Mexico, defeated but lucky to be alive.

One hundred fifty years will pass before a permanent settlement is finally established on the Island. Until then the place will be visited rarely, usually by a local tribe known as the Panzacola. The Island will see many significant events over time, but this first, ultimately doomed attempt to settle

ABOVE: A mid fifteenth century Spanish coin possibly from the Luna expedition, was found in an indian burial. Note the hole made for a necklace.

RIGHT: This early map depicts the "Isle de Saint Rose" about 1719

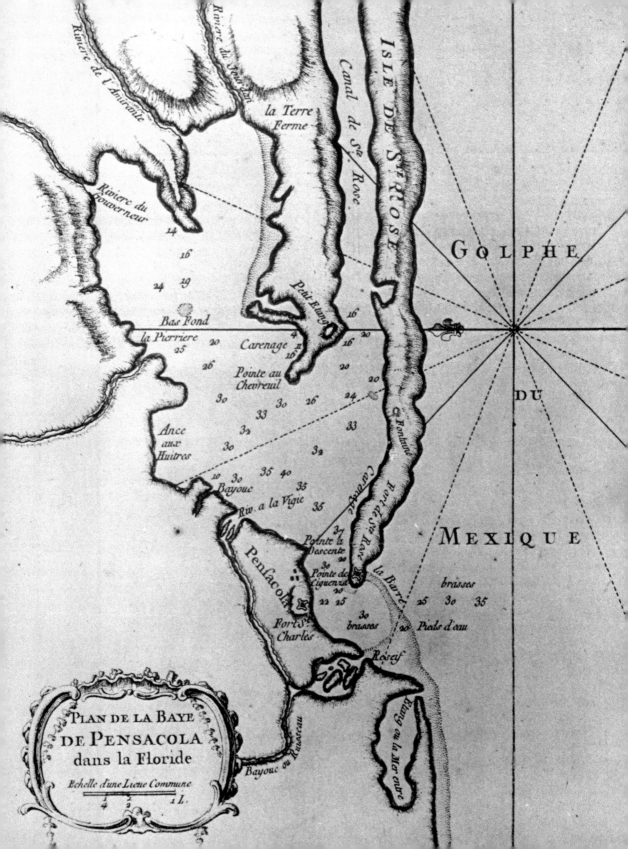

Rivière de l'Amirauté

Rivière du Jourdan

la Terre Ferme

ISLE DE S.te ROSE

Canal de S.te Rose

Rivière du Gouverneur

14

16

24   19

Bas Fond

la Pierriere   20

25

26

Carenage

Pointe au Chevreuil

Ance aux Huitres

Petit Etang

4

11

16

16

16

20

20

20

30   30   26   24

33

32   33

30   32

10 30 35 40

Bayouc   35

Riv. a la Vigie   35

G.de Fontaine

Port de S.te Rose

Canal d'Est

Pointe a Descente

20

30   20

Pointe de Ciguenza

22 25

Pensacola

Fort S.t Charles

30 brasses

la Barre

37

brasses

25   30   35

30   20 Pieds d'eau

Recief

Etang ou la Mer entre

Bayouc ou Rousseau

GOLPHE

DU

MEXIQUE

PLAN DE LA BAYE
DE PENSACOLA
dans la Floride

Echelle d'une Lieue Commune
4   2   1 L.

her serves as a cautionary tale about good intentions and bad weather. It also illustrates that, in the summer of 1559, the Island of Saint Rose was the site of the first colonial settlement in all of North America.

FORT PICKENS - A SHORT HISTORY

In 1821 Florida was ceded to the United States by Spain. The new acquisition was vast and vulnerable; over 2,000 miles of coastline made defense difficult for military planners. From France one of Napoleon's own engineers, Simon Bernard, was enlisted to head a fortification program that would continue for over 60 years.

Pensacola Bay was selected as the principal site for the U.S. Depot on the Gulf Coast. General Bernard chose Santa Rosa Island as the primary location for a series of four forts to defend the bay.

Work on Fort Pickens itself began in 1829. Five years

A Perspective View of Pensacola.
1 The Fort. 2 The Church. 3 The Governors House. 4 The Commandants House. 5 A Well. 6 A Bunga.

ABOVE: An engraving made in 1743 showing the Spanish village on Santa Rosa Island. (Author's Collection)

and 20 million bricks later the Island stronghold was complete, mounting over 100 canon that could be aimed at any vessel attempting to enter the bay.

THE CIVIL WAR ERA

Ironically Fort Pickens was held by the Union throughout the Civil War, and the only real action seen at the fort came during that conflict.

In October of 1861 a Confederate force, some 1,500 strong, attempted to take Fort Pickens in what came to be known as the "Battle of Santa Rosa Island." That assault failed and the Confederates suffered 87 casualties before withdrawing back to the mainland.

GERONIMO AT FORT PICKENS

Advances in weaponry made Fort Pickens obsolete in the late 19th century, and it came to be used mainly as a training and

ABOVE: Construction floor plan of Fort Pickens.

RIGHT: Scores of masonry arches give structural strength to Fort Pickens. Much of the craftsmanship was performed by slave labor.

practice range. But Fort Pickens gained notoriety one more time in 1886 when the infamous Geronimo, along with a band of his Apache warriors, were brought to the Island. This came about after an intense lobbying effort by Pensacola boosters who sought to create the area's first tourist attraction. During their eighteen month imprisonment, the Apaches drew thousands of curious visitors from around the country and the world. Apparently, Geronimo quickly became wise to the tourist trade. The story goes that he would offer buttons from his coat for sale to eager visitors. Each night he would then have one of his three wives sew fresh buttons on, and be ready for a new group of souvenir seekers!

Today Fort Pickens and miles of surrounding area are protected as a national treasure. The Gulf Islands region is the largest preserve in the entire National Seashore system.

Courtesy of the Pensacola Historical Society

LEFT: Curved stairs leading to a lookout atop Fort Pickens.

HISTORICAL HIGHLIGHTS

Santa Rosa Island aerial photo
taken after hurricane, 1916

1539	1559	1693	1723	1743	1752
Maldonado enters Pensacola Bay seeking a rendezvous point with Soto.	Luna expedition arrives August 14th; a hurricane hits days later.	Pez and Reina return to the bay.	A new settlement is built on the Island.	Artist Dom Serres sketches the Island settlement for an English publication; first known reproduction of the Island. (pg. 95)	Hurricane destroys most of the Island settlement.

Pensacola Beach, 1890's

Casino Beach, circa
late 1930's

1829	1861	1886	1916	1932
Construction of Fort Pickens begins on the Island.	Confederates attack Fort Pickens in the Battle of Santa Rosa Island.	Geronimo imprisoned at Fort Pickens.	First known aerial photograph of the Island, taken as part of hurricane damage survey.	First bridge links the Island to Gulf Breeze; modern era begins.

Prints of your favorite photos
from this book are available
from TERRA NOVA Publishing.
(904) 932-9773

FOR FURTHER INFORMATION

The following organizations can provide helpful
information If you're planning a visit to Santa
Rosa Island:

Gulf Islands National Seashore
(904) 934-2600
Santa Rosa Island Authority
(904) 932-2257
Pensacola Beach Visitor Information Center
1-800-635-4803
Emerald Coast Convention & Visitor's Bureau
1-800-322-3319

The titles below were used for reference in the
preparation of this book. For those interested
in an in-depth look at the Island's history, we
recommend these excellent volumes:

National Seashores: *The Story Behind the
Scenery*, Connie Toops, (KC Publications).

Gulf Islands: *The Sands of all Time*,
Jesse Earle Bowden, (Eastern National).

Audubon Society Nature Guides: *Atlantic &
Gulf Coasts*, William Amos, (Alfred A. Knopf, Inc).

Pensacola: *The Deep Water City*, Lucas and
Linda Ellsworth, (Continental Heritage Press).

I S L A N D

O R D E R   F O R M

Please send me_____copies of The Island @ $29.95 each.

Total Amount:_____
Free shipping in the continental United States.

Name:_____

Address_____

City:_____

State/Zip:_____

Florida residents add 7% sales tax. Allow 3-4 weeks for delivery.
Please send check or money order to: TERRA NOVA PUBLISHING
24 Harbourtown Village
Gulf Breeze, FL 32561

Prints of your favorite photos from this book are also available from **TERRA NOVA Publishing**.
Phone orders for prints and book: **(904) 932-9773**

I S L A N D

O R D E R   F O R M

Please send me_____copies of The Island @ $29.95 each.

Total Amount:_____
Free shipping in the continental United States.

Name:_____

Address_____

City:_____

State/Zip:_____

Florida residents add 7% sales tax. Allow 3-4 weeks for delivery.
Please send check or money order to: TERRA NOVA PUBLISHING
24 Harbourtown Village
Gulf Breeze, FL 32561

Prints of your favorite photos from this book are also available from **TERRA NOVA Publishing**.
Phone orders for prints and book: **(904) 932-9773**

I S L A N D

O R D E R   F O R M

Please send me_____copies of The Island @ $29.95 each.

Total Amount:_____
Free shipping in the continental United States.

Name:_____

Address_____

City:_____

State/Zip:_____

Florida residents add 7% sales tax. Allow 3-4 weeks for delivery.
Please send check or money order to: TERRA NOVA PUBLISHING
24 Harbourtown Village
Gulf Breeze, FL 32561

Prints of your favorite photos from this book are also available from **TERRA NOVA Publishing**.
Phone orders for prints and book: **(904) 932-9773**

I S L A N D

O R D E R   F O R M

Please send me_____copies of The Island @ $29.95 each.

Total Amount:_____
Free shipping in the continental United States.

Name:_____

Address_____

City:_____

State/Zip:_____

Florida residents add 7% sales tax. Allow 3-4 weeks for delivery.
Please send check or money order to: TERRA NOVA PUBLISHING
24 Harbourtown Village
Gulf Breeze, FL 32561

Prints of your favorite photos from this book are also available from **TERRA NOVA Publishing**.
Phone orders for prints and book: **(904) 932-9773**